VOGUE KNITTING

SCARVES
TWO

VOGUE KNITTING

SCARVES TWO

SIXTH&SPRING BOOKS
NEW YORK

SIXTH&SPRING BOOKS

233 Spring Street
New York, New York 10013

Library of Congress Cataloging-in-Publication Data

Vogue knitting scarves two / [book editor, Trisha Malcolm].--1st ed.
    p. cm. -- (Vogue knitting on the go!)
    ISBN 1-931543-32-1
    1. Knitting--Patterns. 2. Scarves. I. Title: Scarves two. II. Title: Vogue knitting scarves
    2. III. Malcolm, Trisha, 1960- IV. Vogue knitting international. V. Series.

TT825 .V645 2003
746.43'0462--dc21   2002044559

Manufactured in China

1 3 5 7 9 10 8 6 4 2

First Edition

TABLE OF CONTENTS

INTRODUCTION

Most of us spend our lives juggling work, family and friends, running endless errands and participating in countless activities. Knitting—a relaxing and stress-relieving activity—provides a welcome respite from the hectic world around us.

Scarves make the ultimate fashion statement and often add a personal touch of whimsy to any wardrobe. Whether your taste leans towards the light and lacy or the more casual and sporty, Scarves Two brims with a collection of memorable designs to suit everybody, every occasion and every season. And they're perfect for using up those odds and ends of yarn or splurging on precious luxury yarns without straining your budget.

Accessories are seasonless treasures and you don't have to wait for the first blast of Arctic air to don a sumptuous new scarf. With patterns ranging from beginner to advanced incorporating cables, colorwork or fine lace, fashioning a scarf for a family member or friend can open endless design possibilities. The selection of yarns, stitches and embellishments is mind-boggling. A project you once started at the checkout line or at the kids' karate practice eventually becomes an exquisite hand-made creation stitched with love.

From watching the evening news and chatting on the phone to picking up your kids from soccer practice and passing time in the waiting room of a doctor's office, lost moments often can be converted into productive little windows of opportunity to slip in a row or two. If you're looking for a quick knit and portable project, scarves are the ideal solution.

So stop by your favorite yarn shop, pick up something exquisite, tuck your needles in your bag and get ready to **KNIT ON THE GO!**

THE BASICS

Scarves have been around since the beginning of time and have taken many forms and shapes in cultures the world over. As a result, they've become one of the oldest and most enduring accessories. In its early existence, scarves were often worn around the waist, neck, head, shoulders or entire body for both warmth and modesty. In fact, men in the sixteenth century originally wore them as sashes or belts that were slung across the body from shoulder to shoulder or shoulder to hip to serve as pouches for carrying small articles. The scarf gradually evolved to being more than just a practical and functional item of clothing, and by the nineteenth century, the neckscarf became a fashion statement. Even today, scarves remain as one of the hottest and sought-after fashion accessories for both men and women. Whether you're making a making a personal statement, accessorizing an outfit, or just keeping warm on a brisk day, the varieties of scarves available are as varied as the yarns, colors and patterns they are fashioned in.

Scarves are a perfect introduction to knitting for many beginners. They are easy and quick to stitch, which makes for instant gratification. For more experienced knitters, a scarf lends itself to endless opportunities to explore new stitch patterns, experiment with cables, incorporate colorwork patterns and use up those odds and ends from your yarn stash. It even affords you the opportunity to splurge on a small scale on an exquisite cashmere or angora yarn without draining your bank account. A scarf is one of the simplest yet the most expressive projects you could possibly select to knit.

This book provides a well-rounded selection of scarves to stimulate your imagination and cultivate your creative side. Whether you knit a scarf to express yourself or as a gift for a friend, you're certain to find endless hours of pleasure in knitting these truly unique projects from *Scarves Two*.

SCARF STYLES
Scarf
Meant to wrap the neck for warmth, this flat, rectangular piece is usually no more

GAUGE

Most scarf patterns don't rely on a perfect fit as a knitted garment would, but it is still important to knit a gauge swatch. Without correct gauge a colorwork pattern (such as the Reindeer Fringed Scarf on page 67) may become distorted. The type of needles used—straight or circular, wood or metal—will influence gauge, so knit your swatch with the needles you plan to use for the project. Measure gauge as illustrated here. Try different needle sizes until your sample measures the required number of stitches and rows. *To get fewer stitches to the inch/cm, use larger needles; to get more stitches to the inch/cm, use smaller needles.*

It's a good idea to keep your gauge swatch in order to test blocking and cleaning methods.

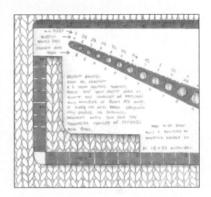

than twelve inches (30.5 centimeters) wide, and three to six feet (or meters) in length, but can be any dimension you choose.

Shawl

Rectangular, semi-circular, or triangular in shape, often with a fringed border, the shawl is worn draped around the shoulders. When made in luxurious yarns and patterns, it becomes an elegant evening accessory.

Stole

Wider and longer than a scarf, the stole wraps the torso for warmth. It is a fashionable substitute for a lightweight jacket or sweater. See our Openwork Pattern Stole on page 40.

FINISHING

Because scarves are frequently knit in one piece, finishing of the garment must be considered from the onset. We've included some helpful hints to remember when beginning your scarf project.

I Because the back-side of the fabric will be seen when the scarf is wrapped around your body, you must be ready for the reverse side to be on display. Think about using a stitch that is reversible, or one which looks good on both sides.

2 Consider adding border stitches to your scarf so that the garment has a built-in finish (many border stitches will also help the fabric lie flat).

3 When adding a new yarn, be careful to do so in a place where you can easily weave the end into the garment, as there is frequently no "wrong side" on a scarf.

4 Knitting a scarf twice as wide as necessary is one way to ensure extra warmth as well as a clean finish. Just fold over and sew up along the seam for a cozy and completely reversible wrap.

5 Consider adding a luxurious fabric lining or a purchased scarf as an elegant accent to your fine handwork for added warmth or to cover up the wrong side.

YARN SELECTION

For an exact reproduction of the scarf photographed, use the yarn listed in the materials section of the pattern. We've selected yarns that are readily available in the U.S. and Canada at the time of printing.

The Resources list on page 94 provides addresses of yarn distributors. Contact them for the name of a retailer in your area.

YARN SUBSTITUTION

You may wish to substitute yarns. Perhaps a spectacular yarn matches your new coat, maybe you view small-scale projects as a chance to incorporate leftovers from your yarn stash, or the yarn specified may not be available in your area. Scarves allow you to be as creative as you like, but you'll need to knit to the given gauge to obtain the knitted measurements with the substitute yarn (see "Gauge" on page 11). Make pattern adjustments where necessary. Be sure to consider how different yarn types (chenille, mohair, bouclé, etc.) will affect the final appearance of your scarf, and how they will feel against your skin. Also take fiber care

POM-POMS

1 Following the template, cut two circular pieces of cardboard.

2 Hold the two circles together and wrap the yarn tightly around the cardboard several times. Secure and carefully cut the yarn.

3 Tie a piece of yarn tightly between the two circles. Remove the cardboard and trim the pom-pom to the desired size.

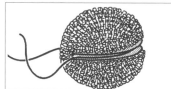

into consideration, some yarns can be machine or hand washed, others will require dry cleaning.

To facilitate yarn substitution, *Vogue Knitting* grades yarn by the standard stitch gauge obtained in Stockinette stitch. You'll find a grading number in the "Materials" section of the pattern, immediately following the fiber type of the yarn. Look for a substitute yarn that falls into the same category. The suggested needle size and gauge on the ball band should be comparable to that on the Yarn Symbols chart on page 16.

After you've successfully gauge-swatched a substitute yarn, you'll need to figure out how much of the substitute yarn the project requires. First, find the total length of the original yarn in the pattern (multiply number of balls by yards/meters per ball). Divide this figure by the new yards/meters per ball (listed on the ball band). Round up to the next whole number. The answer is the number of balls required.

FOLLOWING CHARTS

Charts provide a convenient way to follow colorwork, lace, cable and other stitch

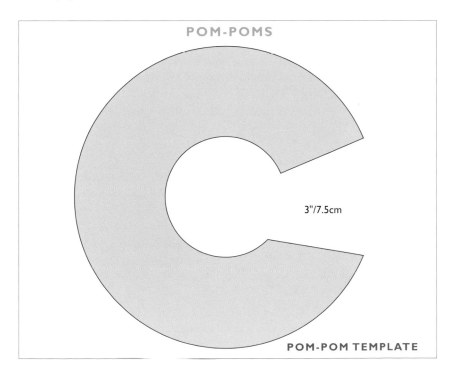

POM-POMS

3"/7.5cm

POM-POM TEMPLATE

patterns at a glance. *Vogue Knitting* stitch charts utilize the universal knitting language of "symbolcraft." Unless otherwise indicated, read charts from right to left on right side (RS) rows and from left to right on wrong side (WS) rows, repeating any stitch and row repeats as directed in the pattern. Posting a self-adhesive note under your working row is an easy way to keep track of your place on a chart.

COLORWORK KNITTING

Two main types of colorwork are explored in this book.

Intarsia

Intarsia is accomplished with separate bobbins of individual colors. This method is ideal for large blocks of color or for motifs that aren't repeated close together. When changing colors, always pick up the new color and wrap around the old color to prevent holes.

Stranding

When motifs are closely placed, colorwork is accomplished by stranding along two or more colors per row, creating "floats" on the wrong side of the fabric. When using this method, twist yarns on WS to prevent holes and strand loosely to keep knitting from puckering.

Note that yarn amounts have been calculated for the colorwork method suggested in the pattern. Knitting a stranded pattern with intarsia bobbins will take less yarn, while stranding an intarsia pattern will require more yarn.

BLOCKING

Blocking is the best way to shape pattern pieces and smooth knitted edges. However, some yarns, such as chenilles and ribbons, do not benefit from blocking. Choose a blocking method according to the yarn care label and, when in doubt, test-block on your gauge swatch.

Wet Block Method

Using rust-proof pins, pin scarf to measurements on a flat surface and lightly dampen using a spray bottle. Allow to dry before removing pins.

Steam Block Method

Pin scarf to measurements with wrong side of knitting facing up. Steam lightly, holding the iron 2"/5cm above the work. Do not press the iron onto the knitting, as it will flatten the stitches.

CARE

Refer to the yarn label for the recommended cleaning method. Many of the scarves in the book can be washed by hand (or in the machine on a gentle or wool cycle) in lukewarm water with a mild detergent. Do not agitate, and don't soak for more than 10 minutes. Rinse gently with tepid water, then fold in a towel and gently press the water out. Lay flat to dry, away from excessive heat and light.

Between two knit stitches: Bring the yarn from the back of the work to the front between the two needles. Knit the next stitch, bringing the yarn to the back over the right-hand needle, as shown.

Multiple yarn overs (two or more): Wrap the yarn around the needle, as when working a single yarn over, then continue wrapping the yarn around the needle as many times as indicated. Work the next stitch of the left-hand needle. On the following row, work stitches into the extra yarn overs as described in the pattern.

FRINGE

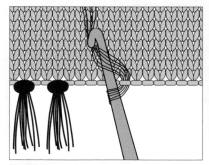

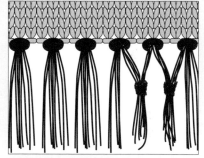

SIMPLE FRINGE: Cut yarn twice desired length plus extra for knotting. On wrong side, insert hook from front to back through piece and over folded yarn. Pull yarn through. Draw ends through and tighten. Trim yarn.

KNOTTED FRINGE: After working a simple fringe (it should be longer to allow for extra knotting), take one half of the strands from each fringe and knot them with half the strands from the neighboring fringe.

KNITTING TERMS AND ABBREVIATIONS

approx approximately

beg begin(ning)

bind off Used to finish an edge and keep stitches from unraveling. Lift the first stitch over the second, the second over the third, etc. (UK: cast off)

cast on A foundation row of stitches placed on the needle in order to begin knitting.

CC contrast color

ch chain(s)

cm centimeter(s)

cont continue(ing)

dc double crochet (UK: tr-treble)

dec decrease(ing)–Reduce the stitches in a row (knit 2 together).

dpn double-pointed needle(s)

foll follow(s)(ing)

g gram(s)

garter stitch Knit every row. Circular knitting: knit one round, then purl one round.

hdc half double crochet (UK: htr-half treble)

inc increase(ing)–Add stitches in a row (knit into the front and back of a stitch).

k knit

k2tog knit 2 stitches together

LH left-hand

lp(s) loop(s)

m meter(s)

M1 make one stitch–With the needle tip, lift the strand between last stitch worked and next stitch on the left-hand needle and knit into the back of it. One stitch has been added.

MC main color

mm millimeter(s)

YARN SYMBOLS

① **Fine Weight**
(29-32 stitches per 4"/10cm)
Includes baby and fingering yarns, and some of the heavier crochet cottons. The range of needle sizes is 0-4 (2-3.5mm).

② **Lightweight**
(25-28 stitches per 4"/10cm)
Includes sport yarn, sock yarn, UK 4-ply, and lightweight DK yarns. The range of needle sizes is 3-6 (3.25-4mm).

③ **Medium Weight**
(21-24 stitches per 4"/10cm)
Includes DK and worsted, the most commonly used knitting yarns. The range of needle sizes is 6-9 (4-5.5mm).

④ **Medium-heavy Weight**
(17-20 stitches per 4"/10cm)
Also called heavy worsted or Aran. The range of needle sizes is 8-10 (5-6mm).

⑤ **Bulky Weight**
(13-16 stitches per 4"/10cm)
Also called chunky. Includes heavier Icelandic yarns. The range of needle sizes is 10-11 (6-8mm).

⑥ **Extra-bulky Weight**
(9-12 stitches per 4"/10cm)
The heaviest yarns available. The range of needle sizes is 11 and up (8mm and up).

no stitch On some charts, "no stitch" is indicated with shaded spaces where stitches have been decreased or not yet made. In such cases, work the stitches of the chart, skipping over the "no stitch" spaces.

oz ounce(s)

p purl

p2tog purl 2 stitches together

pat(s) pattern

pick up and knit (purl) Knit (or purl) into the loops along an edge.

pm place markers–Place or attach a loop of contrast yarn or purchased stitch marker as indicated.

psso pass slip stitch(es) over

rem remain(s)(ing)

rep repeat

rev St st reverse Stockinette stitch–Purl right-side rows, knit wrong-side rows. Circular knitting: purl all rounds. (UK: reverse stocking stitch)

rnd(s) round(s)

RH right-hand

RS right side(s)

sc single crochet (UK: dc-double crochet)

sk skip

SKP Slip 1, knit 1, pass slip stitch over knit 1.

SK2P Slip 1, knit 2 together, pass slip stitch over the knit 2 together.

sl slip–An unworked stitch made by passing a stitch from the left-hand to the right-hand needle as if to purl.

sl st slip stitch (UK: single crochet)

ssk slip, slip, knit–Slip next 2 stitches knitwise, one at a time, to right-hand needle. Insert tip of left-hand needle into fronts of these stitches from left to right. Knit them together. One stitch has been decreased.

sssk Slip next 3 sts knitwise, one at a time, to right-hand needle. Insert tip of left-hand needle into fronts of these stitches from left to right. Knit them together. Two stitches have been decreased.

st(s) stitch(es)

St st Stockinette stitch–Knit right-side rows, purl wrong-side rows. Circular knitting: knit all rounds. (UK: stocking stitch)

tbl through back of loop

tog together

WS wrong side(s)

wyib with yarn in back

wyif with yarn in front

work even Continue in pattern without increasing or decreasing. (UK: work straight)

yd yard(s)

yo yarn over–Make a new stitch by wrapping the yarn over the right-hand needle. (UK: yfwd, yon, yrn)

* = repeat directions following * as many times as indicated.

[ ] = Repeat directions inside brackets as many times as indicated.

For Beginner Knitters

Thick-and-thin wool yarn is played out in shades of red that make up this beginner basic scarf. Jumbo size needles were used by Cara Beckerich in a simple garter stitch creating a loose and open-work fabric.

KNITTED MEASUREMENTS
- Approx 8½" x 60"/21.5cm x 152cm

MATERIALS
- 2 1¾oz/50g hanks (each approx 54yd/ 50m) of Colinette/Unique Kolours *Point 5* (wool⑥) in #47 red multi
- One pair size 35 (19mm) needles *or size to obtain gauge*

GAUGE
7 sts and 7 rows to 4"/10cm over garter st using size 35 (19mm) needles.
Take time to check gauge.

SCARF
With size 35(19mm) needles, cast on 15 sts.
Row 1 Knit.
Rep row 1 for garter st pat until piece measures 60"/152cm from beg. Bind off.

FINISHING
Block very lightly to measurements, do not press.

MENSWEAR STRIPED SCARF

Dot.com

This easy two-color striped scarf is knit in a reversible dot-stitch pattern that is suitable for both men and women. Knit lengthwise in luxurious alpaca yarn with self-fringe in a design by Lipp Holmfeld.

KNITTED MEASUREMENTS

- Approx 9" x 96"/23cm x 244cm

MATERIALS

- 5 2oz/60g balls (each approx 120yd/110m) of Blue Sky Alpacas *100% Alpaca* (alpaca④) in #008 brown (A)
- 2 balls in #003 tan (B)
- Size 5 (3.75mm) circular needle, 40"/100cm long *or size to obtain gauge*

GAUGE

17 sts and 42 rows to 4"/10cm over garter and dot st stripe pat using size 5 (3.75mm) needles.
Take time to check gauge.

Note Scarf is knit lengthwise, that is casting on all sts for total length of scarf. For the self-fringe, an end of 7"/18cm is left at beg and end of every row to be fringed later (This will alleviate all ends being sewn in when scarf is finished).

GARTER AND DOT STITCH PATTERN

Leaving a 7"/18cm end of yarn, with circular needle and A, cast on any number of sts. K1 row with A and cut A leaving a 7"/18cm end of yarn.

Row 1 Leaving a 7"/18cm end of yarn, with B, knit. Cut yarn leaving a 7"/18cm end.
Row 2 Leaving a 7"/18cm end of yarn, with A, knit. Cut yarn leaving a 7"/18cm end.
Row 3 Rep row 1.
Rows 4-8 Rep row 2.
Rep rows 1-8 for garter and dot st pattern.

SCARF

With A, cast on 400 sts. Work in 8-row garter and dot st pat for a total of 11 reps of the 8-row pat. Then, work rows 1-4 once more. Bind off knitwise with A.

FINISHING

Block lightly to measurements.

Fringe

Knot 2 ends of fringe with adjacent 2 ends of fringe. Knot a second time. Trim fringe to 4½"/11.5cm.

Cotton candy

For Experienced Knitters

An openwork lace stitch is worked using a featherweight blend of mohair and silk to create this light and airy scarf. Designed by Lois S. Young.

KNITTED MEASUREMENTS

■ Approx 11" x 58"/28cm x 147cm

MATERIALS

■ 2 .88oz/25g balls (each approx 225yd/205m) of Knit One Crochet Too *Douceur et Soie* (mohair/silk①) in #8248 pink
■ One pair size 3 (3.25mm) needles or size to obtain gauge
■ Blocking wires

GAUGE

21 sts and 30 rows to 4"/10cm over lace pat st (after blocking) foll chart using size 3 (3.25mm) needles.
Take time to check gauge.

Note To achieve the flat and open appearance of the scarf lace pattern as seen in the photo, finished scarf must be well blocked following the finished measurements. Blocking wires are helpful for achieving the best blocked effect.

SCARF

Cast on 59 sts.
Row 1 (WS) Sl 1 st purlwise, k to end.
Rep row 1 for garter st border for a total of 7 rows.
Beg chart pat
Row 1 (RS) Working row 1 of chart, work sts 1-6, then work 6-st rep (sts 7-12) 7 times, work sts 13-23. Cont to foll chart in

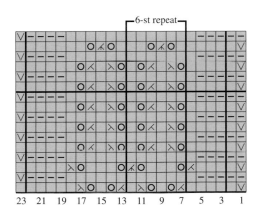

Stitch Key

☐ K on RS, p on WS

− P on RS, k on WS

⋁ Sl 1 st purlwise

⟋ K2tog

⟍ Ssk

⟋ K3tog

◯ Yo

this way, rep rows 1-16 of chart a total of 24 times. Work chart row 1 once more **Next row (WS)** Sl 1 st purlwise, k to end. Rep this row 5 times more. Bind off loosely on WS row.

FINISHING

Lay work flat and pin carefully in place, stretching scarf out severely to finished measurements (or use blocking wires). Mist lightly with water, then leave scarf to dry.

Panels of wavy lace patterning make up the body of this scarf which is trimmed with a sideways knit sawtooth lace edging. Designed by Katherine Hunt.

KNITTED MEASUREMENTS

■ Approx 9" x 60"/ 23cm x 152cm

MATERIALS

■ 6 1¾oz/50g balls (each approx 114yd/ 104m) of Naturally/S.R. Kertzer Ltd. *Luxury DK* (wool/mohair④) in #936 purple
■ One pair size 6 (4mm) needles *or size to obtain gauge*

GAUGE

21 sts and 44 rows to 4"/10cm over lace pat st using size 6 (4mm) needles.
Take time to check gauge.

Notes
1 There is a 3-st seed st border (worked as p1, k1, p1) worked at beg and end of every row along the length of the scarf. To maintain a flat edge to compensate for differing row gauges between the lace pat and these garter st edges, short rows are worked on every pat row 16 as foll: **Row 16** [P1, k1, p1, turn] twice, p1, k1, p1, then work across over the lace body of scarf to last 3 sts, [p1, k1, p1, turn] twice, p1, k1, p1. To maintain a flat edge in this way, no st

wrapping is required.
2 All yo's on RS rows are worked as p o WS rows.

SCARF
Cast on 48 sts.
Row 1 (RS) P1, k1, p1, *k6, p3; rep from * ending last rep p1, k1, p1 instead of p3.
Row 2 and all WS rows P1, k1, p1, *knit the knit sts and purl the purl sts; rep from * to last 3 sts, p1, k1, p1.
Row 3 P1, k1, p1, *yo, k2, ssk, k2, p3; rep from *, ending last rep p1, k1, p1 instead of p3.
Row 5 P1, k1, p1, *k1, yo, k2, ssk, k1, p3; rep from *, ending last rep p1, k1, p1 instead of p3.
Row 7 P1, k1, p1, *k2, yo, k2, ssk, p3; rep from *, ending last rep p1, k1, p1 instead of p3.
Row 9 Rep row 1.
Row 11 P1, k1, p1, *k2, k2tog, k2, yo, p3; rep from *, ending last rep p1, k1, p1 instead of p3.
Row 13 P1, k1, p1, *k1, k2tog, k2, yo, k1, p3; rep from *, ending last rep p1, k1, p1 instead of p3.
Row 15 P1, k1, p1, *k2tog, k2, yo, k2, p3; rep from *, ending last rep p1, k1, p1 instead of p3.
Row 16 See short row borders note, above.
Rep rows 1-16 for lace pat st until piece measures 60"/152cm from beg. Bind off.

Edging

Note Edging is worked lengthwise. Slip all the sl sts knitwise. Cast on 8 sts.

Row 1 *K1, p1; rep from * to end.

Row 2 *P1, k1; rep from * to end.

Row 3 Rep row 1 (for 3 rows in seed st).

Row 4 Sl 1, k2, yo, k2tog, yo twice, k2tog, k1—9 sts.

Row 5 K3, p1, k2, yo, k2tog, k1.

Row 6 Sl 1, k2, yo, k2tog, k1, yo twice, k2tog, k1—10 sts.

Row 7 K3, p1, k3, yo, k2tog, k1.

Row 8 Sl 1, k2, yo, k2tog, k2, yo twice, k2tog, k1—11 sts.

Row 9 K3, p1, k4, yo, k2tog, k1.

Row 10 Sl 1, k2, yo, k2tog, k6.

Row 11 Bind off 3 sts knitwise (1 st rems on RH needle from bind-off), k4, yo, k2tog, k1—8 sts.

Rep rows 4-11 until piece fits lengthwise along one end of scarf, ending with row 10. Bind off 3 sts, p1, [k1, p1] 3 times. Work 1 more row in seed st on 8 sts. Bind off in seed st.

Block scarf to measurements. Sew edging to both ends of scarf.

METALLIC SHIMMER SCARF

Heavy metal mix

Metallic mirror paillettes strung on a novelty yarn are combined with a nubby and metallic yarn to give this scarf all over sparkle appeal. Designed by Margery Winter.

KNITTED MEASUREMENTS

■ Approx 5¼" x 40"/13.5cm x 102cm

MATERIALS

■ 3 .88oz/25g balls (each approx 57yd/52m) of Berroco, Inc. *Jewel FX* (rayon/metallic ③) in #6909 blue (A)

■ 2 .35oz/10g balls (each approx 60yd/55m) of Berroco, Inc. *Mirror FX* (polyester ①) in #9001 gold (B)

■ One pair size 9 (5.5mm) needles *or size to obtain gauge*

■ Size E/4 (3.5mm) crochet hook

GAUGE

18 sts and 20 rows to 4"/10cm over St st using 1 strand each A and B held tog and size 9 (5.5mm) needles.
Take time to check gauge.

Note Work with 1 strand of A and B held tog throughout.

SCARF

With 1 strand A only, cast on 24 sts. Add in 1 strand of B and cont as foll:

Rows 1-6 Knit (for 3 garter ridges).
Work 8"/20.5cm in St st.
Knit 6 rows (for 3 garter ridges).
Work 2½"/6.5cm in St st.
Knit 4 rows (for 2 garter ridges).
Work 6½"/16.5cm in St st.
Knit 6 rows (for 3 garter ridges).
Work 6½"/16.5cm in St st.
Knit 4 rows (for 2 garter ridges).
Work 3"/7.5cm in St st.
Knit 6 rows (for 3 garter ridges).
Work 1½"/4cm in St st.
Knit 4 rows (for 2 garter ridges).
Work 4½"/11.5cm in St st.
Knit 5 rows.
Cut B and with A only, bind off all sts loosely knitwise.

FINISHING

Block scarf to measurements.
Fringe
With A, cut 48 lengths of yarn all measuring 16"/40cm. Using crochet hook, fold fringe in half and pull through each st, going into 2nd ridge of 2 garter ridges (covering the first and last 2 rows of scarf). Allow yarn to untwist naturally for the light fringe effect as in the photo.

Easy twisted cables form the self-scalloping edges of this skinny rib scarf. Designed using a lightweight kid mohair by Irina Poludnenko.

KNITTED MEASUREMENTS

■ Approx 4½" (at widest point) x 73"/ 11.5cm x 185cm

MATERIALS

■ 2 .88oz/25g balls (each approx 149yd/138m) of GGH/Muench Yarns *Soft Kid* (mohair/polyamid/wool⑥) in #71 red
■ One pair size 6 (4mm) needles *or size to obtain gauge*
■ Cable needle (cn)

GAUGE

28 sts and 24 rows to 4"/10cm over rib and cable pat using size 6 (4mm) needles. *Take time to check gauge.*

SCARF

Cast on 6 sts.
Row 1 (RS) Sl 1 st purlwise, k2, p2, p last st.

Row 2 Sl 1 st purlwise, M1, k2, p2, p last st —7 sts.
Row 3 Sl 1 st purlwise, M1, k2, p2, k1, p last st—8 sts.
Row 4 Sl 1 st purlwise, M1, p1, k2, p2, k1, p last st—9 sts.
Cont to work in this way, working M1 at beg of every row after first sl st and p last st of every row, adding inc'd sts in k2, p2 rib until there are 32 sts (23 rows more). Work 1 row even in k2, p2 rib as established. * **Next (cable) row (RS)** Sl 16 sts to cn and hold to *back*, work next 16 sts in rib, work 16 sts from holder in rib.
Work even for 29 rows*. Rep between *'s 12 times more. Rep cable row once more.
Next (dec) row Sl 1 st purlwise, work 2 sts in rib, pass the 2nd st on RH needle over the first st (for dec 1 st), work rib to last st, p1. Rep this row 25 times more—6 sts rem. Bind off in rib.

FINISHING

Block scarf lightly to measurements. If desired, tack scarf at cabled crossing points on WS so that cabled edges lie flat instead of twisting.

INCA PATTERNED SCARF
Peruvian treasure

For Expert Knitters

This design is adopted from an ancient Peruvian textile pattern. The motif incorporates four bold colors set against a dramatic black background. Clever knitted self-tassel cords finish the edges. Designed with knotted self tassel cords by Angela Juergens.

KNITTED MEASUREMENTS

■ Approx 10" x 60"/25.5cm x 152cm

MATERIALS

■ 4 1¾oz/50g balls (each approx 137yd/125m) of Anny Blatt *Merino's* (wool④) in #383 black

■ 1 ball each in #475 lilac, #268 purple, #092 orange and #338 pink

■ Size 7 (4.5mm) circular needles 40"/100cm long *or size to obtain gauge*

GAUGE

21 sts and 34 rows to 4"/10cm over St st using size 7 (4.5mm) needles. Work gauge swatch over St st instead of the pattern. *Take time to check gauge.*

NOTES

1 The colors for this scarf are written out as a color name instead of a letter for easier working of the complex color pattern.

2 K bind off means to bind off knitwise and P bind off means to bind off purlwise.

3 Each row of the pattern is written in three columns: the first and last column are for working the fringes and the center column is for working the center 352 sts.

SCARF

With black, cast on 412 sts.

FRINGES	SCARF - CENTER 352 STS	OPPOSITE FRINGES
Row 1 K 30 in black;	k in black;	k 30 in black.
Row 2 P 30 in black;	p in black;	p 30 in black.
Row 3 K 30 in black;	k1 in lilac wyib, k1 in black wyib;	k 30 in black.
Row 4 P bind off 30 sts in black;	k1 in lilac wyib, k1 in black wyib;	p 30 in black.
Row 5 K bind off 30 sts in black;	k in lilac;	loop cast-on 25 sts in lilac.
Row 6 P 25 in lilac;	p in lilac;	loop cast-on 25 sts in lilac.
Row 7 K 25 in lilac;	k2 in black wyib, k2 lilac wyib;	k 25 in lilac.
Row 8 P 25 in lilac;	p2 in lilac wyif, p2 in black wyif;	p 25 in lilac.
Row 9 K 25 in lilac;	p in lilac;	k 25 in lilac.
Row 10 P bind off 25 sts in lilac;	k in lilac;	p 25 in lilac.
Row 11 K bind off 25 sts in lilac;	sl 2 wyif, k2 in black;	loop cast-on 40 sts in black.
Row 12 P 40 in black;	k2 p2 in black;	loop cast-on 40 sts in black.
Row 13 K in black;	k in black;	k in black.
Row 14 P 40 in black;	k1 in black wyib, k1 in purple wyib;	p 40 in black.
Row 15 K 40 in black;	p in black;	k 40 in black.
Row 16 P bind off 40 sts in black;	p in black;	p 40 in black.
Row 17 K bind off 40 sts in black;	k 3 in purple, sl 1 wyib;	loop cast-on 30 sts in purple.

FRINGES	SCARF - CENTER 352 STS	OPPOSITE FRINGES
Row 18 P 30 in purple;	sl 1 wyif, k 3 in purple;	loop cast-on 30 sts in purple.
Row 19 K in purple;	k in purple ;	k in purple.
Row 20 P 30 in purple;	k in purple;	p 30 in purple.
Row 21 K 30 in purple;	k1 in black wyib, k1 in purple wyib;	k30 in purple.
Row 22 P bind off 30 sts in purple;	p1 in purple wyif, p1 in black wyif;	p30 in purple.
Row 23 K bind off 30 sts in purple;	p in black;	loop cast-on 25 sts in black.
Row 24 P 25 in black;	k in black;	loop cast-on 25 sts in black.
Row 25 K 25 in black;	k in black;	k 25 in black.
Row 26 P 25 in black;	k in black;	p 25 in black.
Row 27 K 25 in black;	k2 in black wyib, k2 in orange wyib;	k 25 in black.
Row 28 P bind off 25 sts in black;	p2 in black wyif, p2 in orange wyif;	p 25 in black.
Row 29 K bind off 25 sts in black;	p in orange;	loop cast-on 40 sts in orange.
Row 30 P 40 in orange;	k in orange;	loop cast-on 40 sts in orange.
Row 31 K 40 in orange;	p2 in black wyif, p2 in orange wyif;	k 40 in orange.
Row 32 P 40 in orange;	k2 in orange wyib, k2 in black wyib;	p 40 in orange.
Row 33 K 40 in orange;	k2 in orange wyib, k2 in black wyib;	k 40 in orange.
Row 34 P bind off 40 sts in orange;	k in orange;	p 40 in orange
Row 35 K bind off 40 sts in orange;	k in orange;	loop cast-on 30 sts in black.
Row 36 P 30 in black;	p1 in black, k1 in black;	loop cast-on 30 sts in black.
Row 37 K in black;	k in black;	k in black.
Row 38 P 30 in black;	k in black;	p 30 in black.
Row 39 K 30 in black;	k1 in pink wyib, k1 in black wyib;	k 30 in black.
Row 40 P bind off 30 sts in black;	k in black;	p 30 in black.
Row 41 K bind off 30 sts in black;	k in black;	loop cast-on 25 sts in pink.
Row 42 P 25 in pink;	k3 in pink, sl 1 wyif ;	loop cast-on 25 sts in pink.
Row 43 K 25 in pink;	sl 1 wyib, k3 in pink;	k 25 in pink.
Row 44 P 25 in pink;	k3 in pink, sl 1 wyif ;	p 25 in pink.
Row 45 K in pink;k in pink;	k in pink.	
Row 46 P bind off 25 sts in pink;	k1 in black wyib, k1 in pink wyib ;	p 25 in pink.
Row 47 K bind off 25 sts in pink;	k1 in pink wyib, k1 in black wyib;	loop cast-on 40 sts in black.
Row 48 P 40 in black;	p in black;	loop cast-on 40 sts in black.
Row 49 K 40 in black;	p in black;	k 40 in black.
Row 50 P 40 in black;	k2 in pink wyib, k2 in black wyib;	p 40 in black.
Row 51 K in black;	k in black;	k in black.
Row 52 P bind off 40 sts in black;	p in black;	p in black.

Row 53 K bind off 40 sts in black; k3 in purple, sl 1 wyib; loop cast on 30 sts in purple.

Row 54 P 30 in purple; sl 1 wyif, k3 in purple; loop cast on 30 sts in purple.

Row 55 K 30 in purple; k1 in black wyib, k1 in purple wyib; k 30 in purple.

Row 56 P 30 in purple; k1 in purple wyib, k1 in black wyib; p 30 in purple.

Row 57 K 30 in purple; p in purple; k30 in purple.

Row 58 P bind off 30 sts in purple; k in purple; p 30 in purple.

Row 59 K bind off 30 sts in purple; k2 in black, sl 2 wyif; loop cast-on 25 sts in black.

Row 60 P 25 in black; p in black; loop cast-on 25 sts in black

Row 61 K 25 in black; p2 in purple wyif, p2 in black wyif; k 25 in black.

Row 62 P 25 in black; k2 in black wyib, k2 in purple wyib; p 25 in black.

Row 63 K in black; k in black; k in black.

Row 64 P bind off 25 sts in black; p in black; p25 in black

Row 65 K bind off 25 sts in black; p1 in orange, sl 1 wyib; loop cast-on 40 sts in orange.

Row 66 P 40 in orange; p1 in orange, k1 in orange; loop cast-on 40 sts in orange.

Row 67 K 40 in orange; k1 in black wyib, k1 in orange wyib; k 40 in orange

Row 68 P 40 in orange; k1 in orange, sl 1 wyib; p 40 in orange.

Row 69 K 40 in orange; p in orange; k 40 in orange.

Row 70 P bind off 40 sts in orange; p1 in black wyif, p1 in orange wyif; p 40 in orange

Row 71 K bind off 40 sts in orange; p1 in black, k1 in black; loop cast-on 30 sts in black.

Row 72 P 30 in black; k in black; loop cast-on 30 sts in black.

Row 73 K in black; k in black; k in black.

Row 74 P 30 in black; k in black; p 30 in black.

Row 75 K 30 in black; k2 in lilac wyib, k2 in black wyib; k 30 in black.

Row 76 P bind off 30 sts in black; p2 in black wyif, p2 in lilac wyif; p 30 in black.

Row 77 K bind off 30 sts in black; p in lilac; loop cast-on 25 sts in lilac.

Row 78 P 25 in lilac; k in lilac; loop cast-on 25 sts in lilac.

Row 79 K 25 in lilac; k1 in black wyib, k1 in lilac wyib; k 25 in lilac.

Row 80 P 25 in lilac; k1 in black wyib, k1 in lilac wyib; p 25 in lilac.

Row 81 K in lilac; k in lilac; k in lilac.

Row 82 P bind off 25 sts in lilac; k in lilac; p 25 in lilac.

Row 83 K bind off 25 sts in lilac; k3 in black, sl 1 wyib; loop cast-on 40 sts in black.

Row 84 P 40 in black; sl 1 wyif, p3 in black; loop cast-on 40 sts in black.

Row 85 K in black; k in black; k in black.

Row 86 P 40 in black; k in black; p 40 in black.

Row 87 K 40 in black; k1 in pink wyib, k1 in black wyib; k 40 in black.

FRINGES	SCARF - CENTER 352 STS	OPPOSITE FRINGES
Row 88 P bind off 40 sts in black;	k1 in black, p1 in black;	p 40 in black.
Row 89 K bind off 40 sts in black;	p in black;	loop cast-on 30 sts in pink.
Row 90 P 30 in pink;	k2 in pink wyif, k2 in black wyif;	loop cast-on 30 sts in pink.
Row 91 K 30 in pink;	p3 in pink, sl 1 wyib;	k 30 in pink.
Row 92 P in pink;	p in pink;	p in pink.
Row 93 K 30 in pink;	k1 in black wyib, k1 in pink wyib;	k 30 in pink.
Row 94 p bind off 30 sts in pink;	k1 in black wyib, k1 in pink wyib;	p 30 in pink.
Row 95 K bind off 30 sts in pink;	k bind off in black.	

FINISHING

Block piece to measurements. Tie knots in fringes.

Garter stitch ridges, shaped ends and face trimmings form the design concept for these whimsical scarves for children. Designed by Amy Bahrt.

KNITTED MEASUREMENTS

- Approx 4½" x 47"/11.5cm x 119cm

MATERIALS

Lamb Scarf

- 1 1¾oz/50g ball (each approx 121yd/110m) of GGH/Muench Yarns *Relax* (alpaca/wool/nylon/acrylic④) in #033 natural (B)
- 1 1¾oz/50g ball (each approx 96yd/87m) of GGH/Muench Yarns *Davos* (wool/acrylic④) in #11 black (A)
- One pair size 7 (4.5mm) needles *or size to obtain gauge*
- Size G/6 (4.5mm) crochet hook
- Two ½"/13mm white buttons (4-holed)

Zebra Scarf

- 1 1¾oz/50g ball (each approx 96yd/87m) of GGH/Muench Yarns *Davos* (wool/acrylic④) each in #11 black (A) and #102 ecru (B)
- One pair size 7 (4.5mm) needles or size to obtain gauge
- Two ⅜"/10mm green buttons

GAUGE

Both scarves
18 sts and 32 rows to 4"/10cm over garter st using size 7 (4.5mm) needles.
Take time to check gauge.

LAMB SCARF

With A, beg at face end, cast on 10 sts.
Row 1 (RS) K2 sts in first st (for inc 1 st), k to last st, inc 1 st in last st. **Row 2** Knit. Rep last 2 rows 4 times more—20 sts. Work even in garter st until piece measures 4¾"/12cm from beg. Cut A. Join B and cont in garter st until piece measures approx 43"/109cm from beg.

Legs
Next row (RS) With B, k6, join 2nd ball of B and bind off center 8 sts, k to end. Work each leg separately for 2½"/6.5cm. Then cut B and join A to each 6-st leg and k 7 rows for foot in A. Bind off knitwise.

FINISHING

Do not block or press flat. Sew on buttons to face as in photo.

Ears
(make 2)
With A, cast on 3 sts.
Row 1 Inc 1 st in first st, k to last st, inc 1 st in last st—5 sts. **Row 2** Purl. Rep last 2 rows once more—7 sts. Work 8 rows more in St st. **Next row (RS)** SKP, k to last 2 sts, k2tog—5 sts. **Next row** Purl. **Next row (RS)** SKP, k1, k2tog—3 sts. Cut yarn and draw through rem 3 sts to form inner curve of ear. Fold ears into curve at cast-on edge and attach to head in 6th row in B above face, leaving 2½"/6.5cm open at center.

ZEBRA SCARF

With A, beg at face end, cast on 10 sts. Work in stripe pat for face for 4¾"/12cm as foll: *k2 rows with A, k2 rows B; rep from * for 4-row garter stripe pat, AT SAME TIME, shape head as foll: **Row 1 (RS)** K2 sts in first st (for inc 1 st), k to last st, inc 1 st in last st. **Row 2** Knit. Rep last 2 rows 4 times more—20 sts. Then cont even in 4-row garter stripe pat until piece measures 4¾"/12cm from beg. Then, work in stripe pat as foll: *K4 rows A, k4 rows B; rep from * for 8-row garter stripe pat until piece measures approx 43"/109cm from beg, end with 4 rows B.

Legs

Note Cont to work 8-row stripe pat while working legs. **Next row (RS)** With B, k6, join 2nd ball of B and bind off center 8 sts, k to end. Work each leg separately for 2½"/6.5cm, ending with 4 rows in B. Then k7 rows with A for each leg for foot. Bind off knitwise.

FINISHING

Do not block or press flat. Sew on buttons to face as in photo.

Ears

(make 2)

Work as for Lamb Scarf's ears. Sew to head as in photo.

Mane

Cut A into eleven 4"/10cm lengths. Using a crochet hook, knot fringe above edges as in photo for mane.

The next wave

Lightweight and bulky weight yarns are paired in any easy openwork pattern with an alternating wave effect. Coordinating ombre colors are used by Norah Gaughan for this stole's design.

KNITTED MEASUREMENTS

■ Approx 20" x 72"/50.5cm x 183cm

MATERIALS

■ 4 3½oz/100g hanks (each approx 76yd/70m) of Artful Yarns *Museum* (wool⑥) in # 3 bright pink/teal multi (A)

■ 2 1¾oz/50g balls (each approx 164yd/148m) of Artful Yarns *Portrait* (mohair/viscose/polyester④) in #103 bright pink/teal multi (B)

■ One pair size 11 (8mm) needles *or size to obtain gauge*

GAUGE

9 sts and 10 rows to 4"/10cm over wave pattern stitch using A and B and size 11 (8mm) needles.
Take time to check gauge.

WAVE PATTERN STITCH

Multiple of 10 sts plus 6
Row 1 (RS) With A, Knit.
Row 2 With B, k1, *k4, wrapping yarn twice around needle for each st, k next 2 sts; wrapping yarn 3 times around needle for each st, k next 2 sts; wrapping yarn twice around needle for each st, k next 2 sts; rep from * 3 times more, k5.
Row 3 With B, knit.
Row 4 With A, knit.
Row 5 With A, knit.
Row 6 With B, *wrapping yarn twice around needle for each st, k next 2 sts; wrapping yarn 3 times around needle for each st, k next 2 sts; wrapping yarn twice around needle for each st, k next 2 sts; k4; rep from * 3 times more, wrapping yarn twice around needle for each st, k next 2 sts; wrapping yarn 3 times around needle for each st, k next 2 sts, wrapping yarn twice around needle for each st, k last 2 sts.
Row 7 With B, knit.
Row 8 With A, knit.
Rep rows 1-8 for wave pat st.

STOLE

With A, cast on 46 sts using single needle cast-on method. Work in wave pat st until piece measures approx 72"/183cm from beg, end with pat row 4 or 8. With A, bind off knitwise.

FINISHING

Block to measurements.

Harlequin romance

Argyle diamonds with pompom trims are worked into a point at each end of this tweed scarf for a unique twist on a classic concept. Designed by Betty Monroe.

KNITTED MEASUREMENTS
- Approx 9"/ x 47"/23cm x 119cm

MATERIALS
- 3 1¾oz/50g balls (each approx 94yd/ 86m) of Adriafil/Plymouth Yarns *Roller* (wool/nylon/rayon⑤) in #68 grey (A)
- 1 ball each in # 61 gold (B), #65 olive (C), #66 navy (D), #64 purple (E) and #67 rust (F)
- Waste yarn (for casting on)
- One pair size 8 (5mm) needles *or size to obtain gauge*
- Size 10 (6mm) circular needle, 40"/ 100cm long

GAUGE
16 sts and 24 rows to 4"/10cm over St st using size 8 (5mm) needles.
Take time to check gauge.

TECHNIQUES USED
The diamonds that are worked on the tips of this scarf are knit in shaped pieces. They are described separately as foll:

Right triangle
(Worked on 6 sts with A)
Row 1 (RS) K5, sl 1.
Row 2 Sl 1, p1, psso, p4—5 sts.

Row 3 K4, sl 1.
Row 4 Sl 1, p1, psso, p3—4 sts.
Row 5 K3, sl 1.
Row 6 Sl 1 p1, psso, p2—3 sts.
Row 7 K2, sl 1.
Row 8 Sl 1, p1, psso, p1—2 sts.
Row 9 K2tog, pull yarn through and fasten off last st.

Left triangle
(Worked on 6 sts with A)
Row 1 (RS) K6.
Row 2 P5, sl 1.
Row 3 SKP, k4—5 sts.
Row 4 P4, sl 1.
Row 5 SKP, k3—4 sts.
Row 6 P3, sl 1.
Row 7 SKP, k2—3 sts.
Row 8 P2, sl 1.
Row 9 SKP, k1—2 sts.
Row 10 P2tog, pull yarn through and fasten off last st.

Half diamond
(Worked on 12 sts with A)
Row 1 (RS) K11, sl 1.
Row 2 Sl 1, p1, psso, p9, sl 1—11 sts.
Row 3 SKP, k8, sl 1 – 10 sts.
Row 4 Sl 1, p1, psso, p7, sl 1—9 sts.
Row 5 SKP, k6, sl 1—8 sts.
Row 6 Sl 1, p1, psso, p5, sl 1—7 sts.
Row 7 SKP, k4, sl 1—6 sts.
Row 8 Sl 1, p1, psso, p3, sl 1—5 sts.
Row 9 SKP, k2, sl 1—4 sts.
Row 10 Sl 1, p1, psso, p1, sl 1—3 sts.
Row 11 SKP, sl 1—2 sts.
Row 12 P2tog, pull yarn through and fasten off last st.

Full diamond

(Worked in B, C, D, E or F picking up and working until there are 12 sts on needle).

With RS facing, and size 8 (5mm) needles, pick up 2 sts in the notch between a triangle and a diamond (or half diamond) or between 2 diamonds (or half diamonds).

Increasing section

Row 1 (WS) P2, pick up 1 st inserting needles under the adjoining slipped st—3 sts.

Row 2 (RS) Sl 1, k2, pick up 1 st inserting needle under the adjoining slipped st—4 sts. Cont to pick up sts in this way until there are 12 sts on needle (8 rows more).

Next row (WS) P11, sl 1.

Decreasing section

Row 1 (RS) SKP, k9, sl 1—11 sts.

Row 2 Sl 1, p1, psso, p8, sl 1—10 sts.

Row 3 SKP, k7, sl 1—9 sts.

Row 4 Sl 1, p1, psso, p6, sl 1—8 sts.

Row 5 SKP, k5, sl 1—7 sts.

Row 6 Sl 1, p1, psso, p4, sl 1—6 sts.

Row 7 SKP, k3, sl 1—5 sts.

Row 8 Sl 1, p1, psso, p2, sl 1—4 sts.

Row 9 SKP, k1, sl 1—3 sts.

Row 10 Sl 1, p1, psso, sl 1—2 sts.

Row 11 K2tog, pull yarn through and fasten off last st.

With size 8 (5mm) needles and waste yarn, cast on 36 sts. Work in St st for 4 rows. Change to A and work in St st for 32"/81cm or approx 192 rows.

Argyle diamond edge

Note See diagram for colors and placement.

Next row (RS) Cont with A, work right triangle over 6 sts, 2 half diamonds over next 24 sts, left triangle over 6 sts. Cont in this way until these triangles and diamonds are completed. Then work 3 full diamonds in F, B and E. Then work 2 full diamonds in D and C. Then work 1 full diamond in B. Fasten off.

Return to sts at beg of row on waste yarn and unravel waste yarn. Work opposite end with argyle diamond edge in same way.

Block to measurements.

Edging

With RS facing, circular needle and A, pick up and k 1 st at point of last diamond in B, pull up a lp under next edge st and knit it; cont in this way along side edge of diamonds to beg scarf in A. Slide sts to opposite end of circular needle so that the sts are on the left point. Bring the other point around and slip 2 sts to RH point. Slip first st over 2nd st to bind off. Cont in this way until 2 sts rem on left front. Slide rem 2 sts to opposite end of circular neede. *Working in the space between the first and second st of side edge, pick up and k 1 st (that is, covering the slipped st), skip 1 st; rep from * until all sts are picked up along side edge of scarf to other diamond edge. Slide sts to opposite end of needle and bind off as before. Cont to work edge in this way around other side edges of diamond points, other side of scarf and first side edge of diamond point. Fasten off.

Pompoms

Make two 3"/7.5cm pompoms using purple (E). Attach to points of scarf.

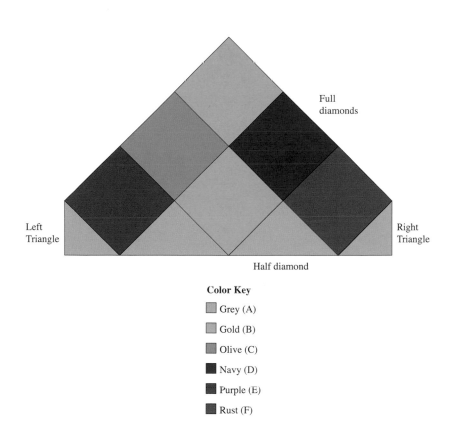

Full diamonds

Left Triangle

Right Triangle

Half diamond

Color Key

- Grey (A)
- Gold (B)
- Olive (C)
- Navy (D)
- Purple (E)
- Rust (F)

For Intermediate Knitters

A classic stitch used in afghans teams standout garter ridges with striped ripples for visual impact. Worked in various colors of a shimmering metallic yarn, this scarf is perfect for evening wear. Designed by Carol Gillis.

KNITTED MEASUREMENTS

■ Approx 9½" x 47"/24cm x 119cm

MATERIALS

■ 3 .88oz/25g balls (each approx 102yd/95m) of Rowan Yarns *Lurex Shimmer* (viscose/polyester②) in #335 brown (A)

■ 1 ball each in #337 aqua (B), #338 purple (C), #333 pewter (D), #331 red (E) and #336 pink (F)

■ One pair size 3 (3.25mm) needles *or size to obtain gauge*

GAUGE

32 sts and 42 rows to 4"/10cm over ripple pat st using size 3 (3.25mm) needles. *Take time to check gauge.*

RIPPLE PATTERN STITCH

(Multiple of 11 sts)

Rows 1-5 With A, knit.

Row 6 (RS) With B, *k2tog, k2, inc 1 st in each of next 2 sts (by k into front and back of each st), k3, SKP; rep from * to end.

Row 7 With B, knit.

Rows 8 and 10 Rep row 6.

Rows 9 and 11 With B, purl.

Row 12 With A, rep row 6.

Rep rows 1-12 for ripple pat st.

SCARF

With A, cast on 77 sts. Foll ripple pat st, rep rows 1-12 and replacing colors in rows 6-11 with C, then D, E and F for a total of 60 rows in color stripe pat.

Note Do not carry colors along side edge of work. Cut colors at end of each color stripe. Work in this way until 8 reps of 12-row stripe pat are completed and scarf measures approx 46½"/118cm. Then with A, k4 rows. Bind off knitwise with A.

FINISHING

Sew in all ends neatly on WS of scarf. Block scarf to measurements.

VIOLET AND CABLE SCARF

English garden

Cable panels alternate with plain stockinette stitch boxes featuring a variety of violets in this pretty lightweight cotton scarf design by Sasha Kagan. One shade of violet is echoed in the multi-knot fringe that trims each end.

KNITTED MEASUREMENTS

Approx 7¼" x 39½"/18.5cm x 100cm

MATERIALS

■ 3 1¾oz/50g balls (each approx 175yd/160m) of Rowan Yarns *Calmer* (cotton/acrylic③) in #464 lt green (A)

■ 1 ball each in #468 plum (C) and #462 pink (E)

■ 1 1¾oz/50g ball (each approx 191yd/175m) of Rowan Yarns *4-Ply Soft* (wool 2) in #375 soft violet (B) – (used double)

■ 1 .88oz/25g ball (each approx 229yd/210m) of Rowan Yarns *Kid Silk Haze* (kid mohair/silk①) in #600 orchid (D) – (used triple)

■ 1 1¾oz/50g ball (each approx 123yd/113m) of Rowan Yarns *Wool Cotton* (cotton/wool③) each in #907 olive (F) and #930 lt olive (G)

■ One pair each sizes 4 and 6 (3.5 and 4mm) needles *or size to obtain gauge*

GAUGE

36 sts and 34 rows to 4"/10cm over pat foll chart using size 6 (4mm) needles. *Take time to check gauge.*

STITCH GLOSSARY

4-st RC Sl next 2 sts to cn and hold to *back*, k2, k2 from cn.

4-st LC Sl next 2 sts to cn and hold to *front*, k2, k2 from cn.

Bobble

(in F or G)

Worked in st as designated on chart, work 4 rows as foll:

Row 1 (RS) K1, p1, k1 into one st, turn.

Row 2 K3, turn.

Row 3 P3, turn.

Row 4 K3tog, turn.

NOTE

When working with A, C, E, F and G, use 1 strand. When working with B, use 2 strands held together. When working with D, use 3 strands held together.

SCARF

With smaller needles and A, cast on 64 sts. K4 rows. Change to larger needles. Work in cable and color st foll chart until 12 reps of 28-row rep of chart have been completed. Piece measures approx 39¼"/99.5cm from beg. Change to smaller needles. With A, k3 rows. Bind off knitwise.

FINISHING

Block scarf to measurements.

Knotted Fringe

Using B, cut 24"/61cm lengths using 4 lengths for each of the 9 fringe at each end of scarf. Knot each of the 9 fringe at the lower edge. Then take 4 strands from one fringe and combine with 4 strands of next fringe at approx ½"/1.5cm from first row of knots. Alternating as in photo, make 3 more rows of knots. Trim evenly.

Stitch and Color Key

☐ K on RS, p on WS

⊟ P on RS, k on WS

▨▨ 4-ST RC

▨▨ 4-ST LC

⬤ Bobble in Olive (F)

⬤ Bobble in Lt. olive (G)

☐ Lt green (A)

◩ Soft violet (B) 2 Strands

■ Plum (C)

■ Orchid (D) 3 Strands

☐ Pink (E)

■ Olive (F)

☐ Lt olive (G)

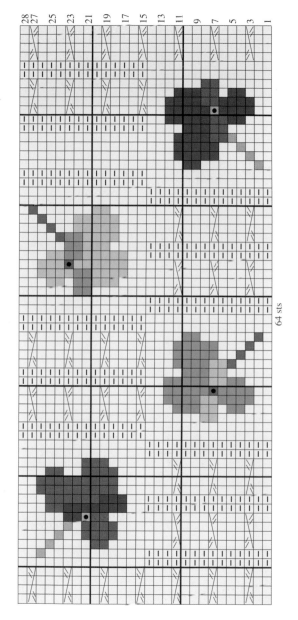

Stripe tease

Four easy seed stitch pieces are knit separately then joined together in alternating strips to create a visually stunning scarf with plenty of textural appeal. A Vogue original.

KNITTED MEASUREMENTS

- Approx 8" x 41"/20.5cm x 104cm

MATERIALS

- 1 1¾oz/50g ball (each approx 65yd/59m) of Classic Elite Yarn *Bazic Wool* each in #2985 orange (A), #2932 burgundy (B), #2958 red (C) and #2995 purple (D)
- One pair size 8 (5mm) needles *or size to obtain gauge*

GAUGE

16 sts and 28 rows to 4"/10cm over seed st pat using size 8 (5mm) needles.
Take time to check gauge.

SEED STITCH PATTERN

(Over an even number of sts)
Row 1 (RS) *K1, p1; rep from * to end.

Row 2 *P1, k1; rep from * to end.
Rep these 2 rows for seed st pat.

SCARF

Stripe

(Make one of each color)
With size 8 (5mm) needles, and color A, cast on 8 sts. Work in seed st for 41"/104cm. Bind off in pattern. Make one more strip each with B, C and D.

FINISHING

Block pieces lightly for easier seaming. Lay out strips as A, B, C and D (see photo). Then sew tog using overcast st to side edge as foll: Join the center B and C strips tog as foll: Leave 4½"/11.5cm at one end open, join for 1"/2.5cm, [leave 6"/15cm open, join for 6"/15cm] twice, leave 6"/15cm open, join for 1"/2.5cm, leave rem 4½"/11.5cm open. Then join A strip to side of B strip to correspond to the center opening (that is, after 5½"/14cm, then at 6"/15cm intervals). Join D strip to C strip foll layout of A strip.

For Intermediate Knitters

These two scarves are knit in garter stitch using a medium weight wool and a small size needle, each with a different bold color combination. The taut and non-stretchable fabric created in this design by Angela Juergens gives added warmth and durability.

KNITTED MEASUREMENTS

■ Approx 9½" x 66½"/24cm x 169cm

MATERIALS

Colorway 1

■ 4 1¾oz/50g balls (each approx 136yd/125m) of Filatura di Crosa/Takhi•Stacy Charles, Inc. *Zara* (wool③) in #6050 red (A)

■ 2 balls in #1703 orange (B)

■ 3 balls in #1503 green (C)

Colorway 2

■ 4 balls in #130 navy (A)

■ 2 balls in #1704 turquoise (B)

■ 3 balls in #1503 green (C)

Both colorways

■ One pair size 4 (3.5mm)needle *or size to obtain gauge*

GAUGE

25 sts and 54 rows to 4"/10cm over garter st using size 4 (3.5mm) needles.
Take time to check gauge.

Notes

1 Work each block of color with a separate ball of yarn. Twist yarns tog at color changes to avoid holes in work.

2 When foll chart for color block patterns in garter st, each square represents 1 stitch and 2 rows (2 rows=1 ridge).

SCARF

With size 4 (3.5mm) needles and A, cast on 62 sts.
Row 1 (RS) P1, k to end.
Row 2 P1, k to end. Rep these 2 rows for garter st, AT SAME TIME, foll chart rows 1-872 for desired colorway.Bind off.

FINISHING

Block scarves lightly to measurements.

Color Key

■ Red (A)

■ Orange (B)

□ Green (C)

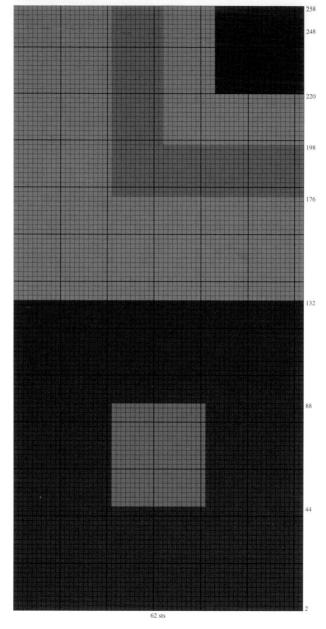

258

248

220

198

176

132

88

44

2

62 sts

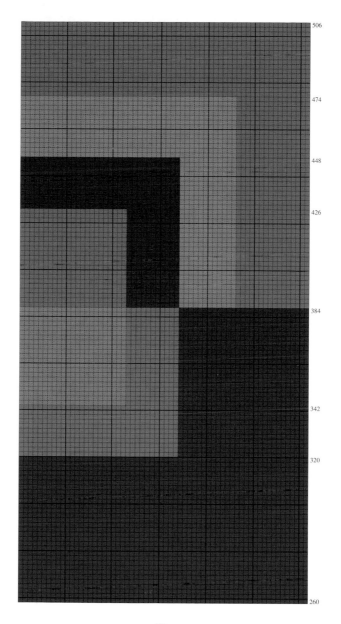

Color Key

- Red (A)
- Orange (B)
- Green (C)

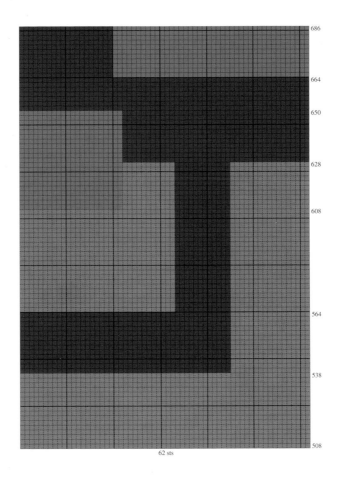

62 sts

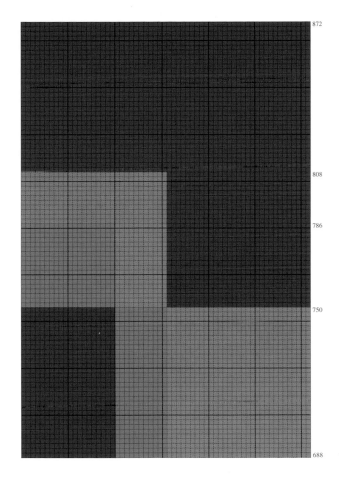

808

786

750

688

872

COLORWAY 2

Color Key

■ Navy (A)

■ Turquoise (B)

■ Green (C)

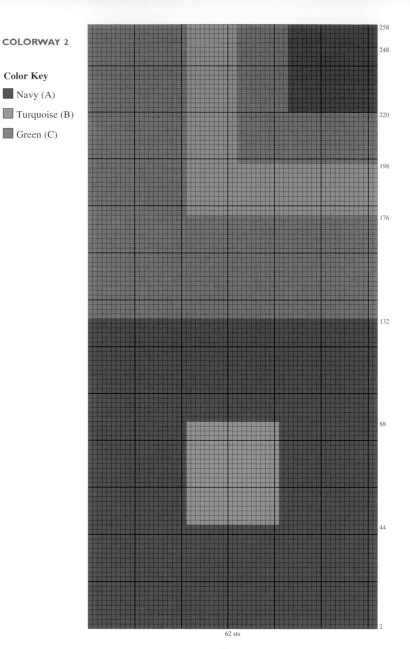

62 sts

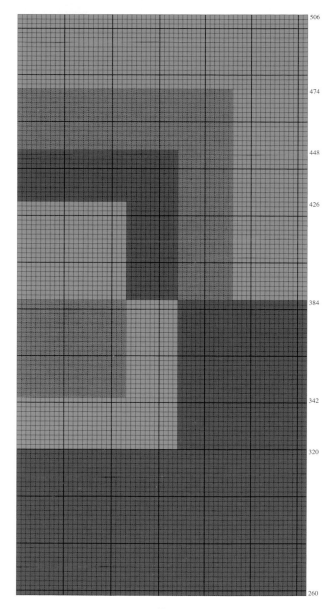

506

474

448

426

384

342

320

260

Color Key

- ■ Navy (A)
- ■ Turquoise (B)
- ■ Green (C)

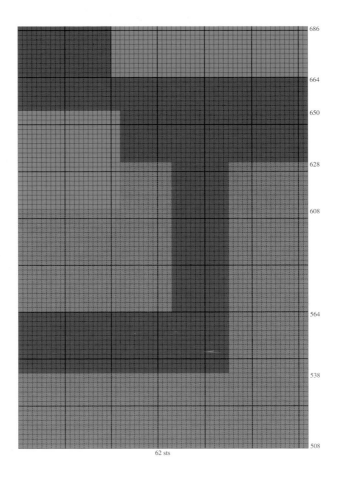

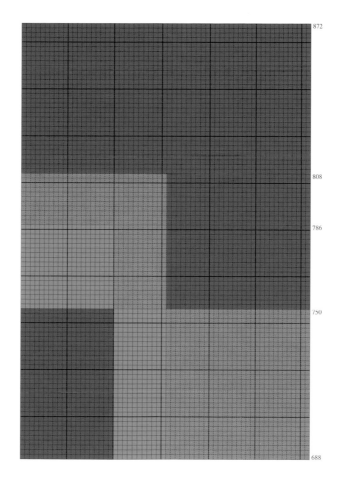

872

808

786

750

688

ARAN SCARF
Cable connection

For Intermediate Knitters

Smooth flowing center diamond cable crossing panel bordered by ribs, creates a hightly textured woven appearance on this casually elegant scarf fashioned in luxurious cashmere. Designed by Veronica Manno.

KNITTED MEASUREMENTS

- Approx 7" x 53"/18cm x 134.5cm

MATERIALS

- 2 3½oz/100g skeins (each approx 165yd/152m) of Trendsetter Yarns *Dali* (cashmere ④) in #169 purple
- One pair size 9 (5.5mm) needles *or size to obtain gauge*
- Cable needle (cn)

GAUGE

24 sts and 22 rows to 4"/10cm over rib and cable pat foll chart using size 9 (5.5mm) needles.

Take time to check gauge.

STITCH GLOSSARY

4-ST RPC Sl next st to cn and hold to *back*, k next 3 sts, p1 from cn.

4-ST LPC Sl next 3 sts to cn and hold to *front*, p next st, k3 from cn.

6-ST RC Sl next 3 sts to cn and hold to *back*, k next 3 sts, k3 from cn.

6-ST LC Sl next 3 sts to cn and hold to *front*, k next 3 sts, k3 from cn.

SCARF

Cast on 42 sts. Beg with row 1, foll chart through row 6. Then rep rows 7-42 (36-row repeat) a total of 8 times. Then work rows 43-51 once. Bind off in rib.

FINISHING

Block to measurements being sure not to flatten rib.

Stitch Key

☐ K on RS, p on WS   4-St LPC

☐ P on RS, k on WS   6-St RC

4-St RPC   6-St LC

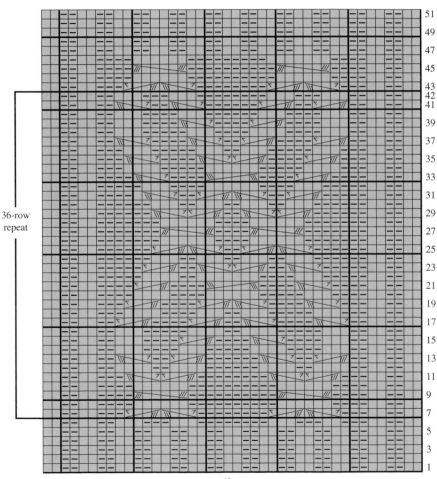

36-row repeat

42 sts

REINDEER FRINGED SCARF
The Great Outdoors

Exra-bulky yarn combines with jumbo needles to make up this chunky stole or scarf in an easy two-color motif. A mere 25 stitches across knits up quickly in a design by Mari Lynn Patrick.

KNITTED MEASUREMENTS

■ Approx 11½" x 78"/29cm x 198cm

MATERIALS

■ 5 3½oz/100g hanks (each approx 57yd/52m) of Classic Elite Yarns *Waterspun Weekend* (wool⑥) in #2773 heather brown (A)

■ 3 hanks in #2783 black (B)

■ One pair size 17 (12mm) needles *or size to obtain gauge*

GAUGE

8 sts and 10 rows to 4"/10cm over St st foll chart using size 17 (12mm) needles. *Take time to check gauge.*

Notes

I When working reindeer motif, work separate blocks of color with separate balls or bobbins, twisting yarns at color changes to avoid holes. When working other motifs foll chart, carry yarn at back of work.

2 The yarn amount uses up all of the A yarn including fringe. Use B for fringe if you do not have sufficient yarn in A.

SCARF

With A, cast on 25 sts.
Row I (RS) K1, p1, k21, p1, k1.
Row 2 P1, k1, p21, k1, p1.
Rep these two rows throughout, work even with A for 2 rows more.

Beg chart
Row I (RS) With A, k1, p1, work row 1 of chart over 21 sts, with A, p1, k1.
Row 2 With A, p1, k1, work row 2 of chart over 21 sts, with A, k1, p1.
Cont to foll chart in this way, working first and last 2 sts with A as before, through row 54. Then rep rows 43-54 only 9 times more. Then work rows 55-70 of chart. Bind off.

FINISHING

Lay scarf flat and block to measurements on WS. Weave in ends over several sts to prevent from raveling.

Fringe
For each fringe, cut 4 lengths of yarn 20"/50cm each. Knot 7 fringe from WS- along each lower edge of scarf. Lay on a flat surface and trim evenly.

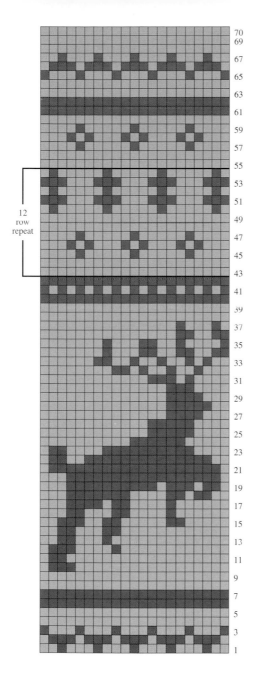

70
69
67
65
63
61
59
57
55
53
51
49
47
45
43
41
39
37
35
33
31
29
27
25
23
21
19
17
15
13
11
9
7
5
3
1

12
row
repeat

Color Key

Heather brown (A)

Black (B)

YARN MIX SCARF

Rhythm and blues

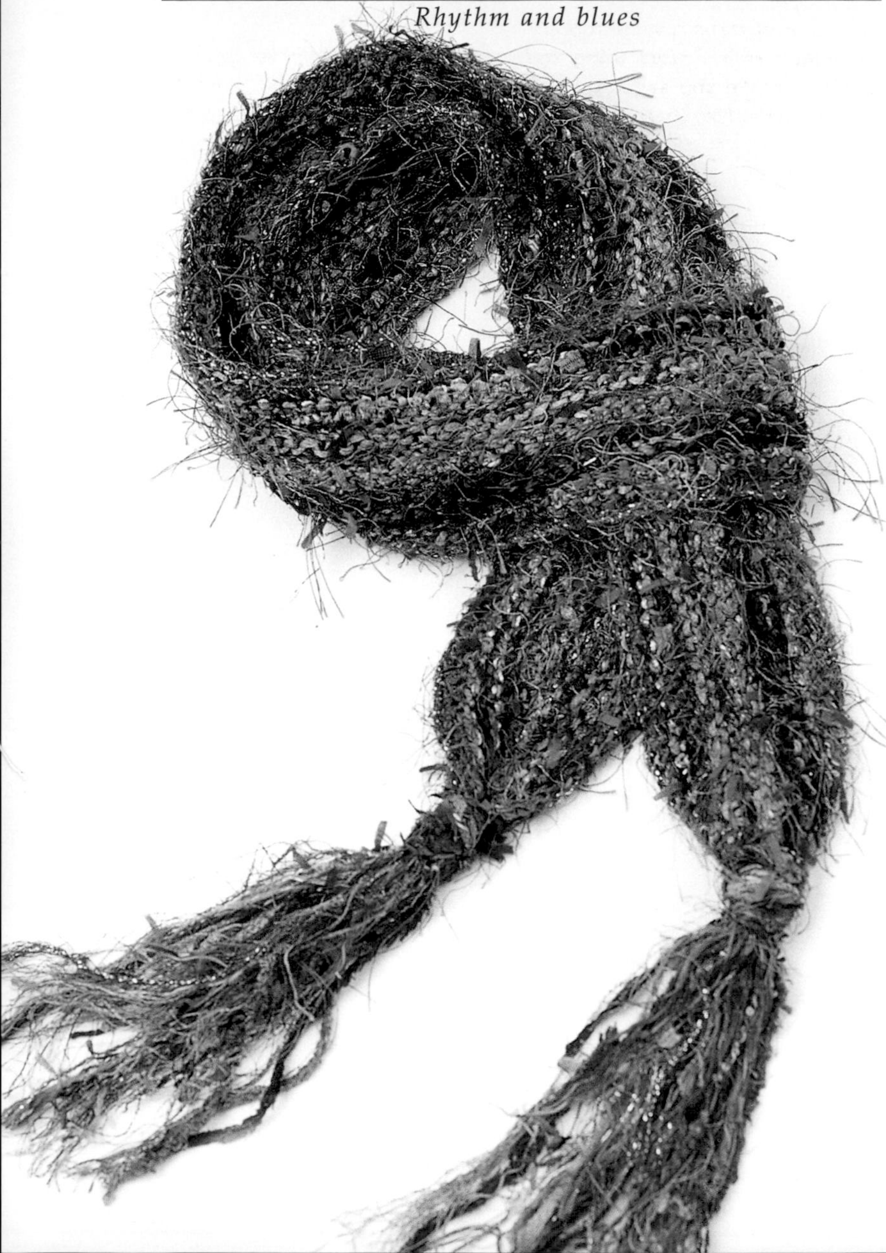

An allover mix of yarns is used to make a truly unique styled scarf using the yarn itself to make the self fringe on every row. Designed by Sharon O' Brien in a mix of plain, novelty, metallic, slub and fur textured yarns.

■ Approx 5" x 50"/12.5cm x 127cm

Use a mix of yarns totaling 323-369yd/315-360m in shades of blue and green in the foll types and suggestions:
A-green/blue variegated worsted weight (④) textured yarn (suggested: Cherry Tree Hill Yarns *Ballerina*)
B-multi-color slub yarn, worsted weight (④) rayon and cotton (suggested: Crystal Palace Yarns *Waikiki*)
C-fur-type chenille yarn, heavy worsted weight (⑤) (suggested: Berroco, Inc. Yarns *Chinchilla*)
D-multiple-ply metallic yarn, worsted weight (④) (suggested: Plymouth Yarns *Goldrush*)
E-very fine (②) multicolor eyelash type yarn (suggested: Lane Borgosesia *Fur* or Berroco, Inc. Yarns *Zap*)
■ One pair size 7 (4.5mm) needles *or size to obtain gauge*
■ Size 7 (4.5mm) circular needle, 29"/74cm long
■ Size H/8 (5mm) crochet hook

16 sts and 42 rows to 4"/10cm over welt pat st using a variety of yarns and size 7 (4.5mm) needles.
Take time to check gauge.

Note To create the scarf as in the photo, a new color and type of yarn is worked in each row leaving yarn at both ends to create the fringe. The length of the fringe is as desired. When using the finer weight, yarn may need to be doubled to achieve the right look.

Rows 1, 2 and 3 Knit.
Row 4 Purl.
Rep these 4 rows for welt pat st.

Leaving approx 10"/25.5cm for fringe, with desired yarn, chain approx 200 sts, leaving 10"/25.5 cm for opposite fringe. Being sure that chain is fairly loose, pick up and k 1 st in each ch (for chain cast-on). With circular needle, knit 1 row. Cut yarn with fringe end. Leaving 10"/25.5 cm for fringe (and knot each new yarn using a single knot method), cont to work the 4-row welt pat st, changing to a new yarn on each row and cont in this way until 36 rows in welt pat st are completed. Bind off loosely (being sure that edge is as flexible as the cast-on edge).

Block lightly. Make a large overhand knot at each end. Trim fringe to a tapered point, if desired.

Lap of luxury

Easy seed stitch forms the background for this short scarf that wraps your neck in fine mohair with an opulent rabbit fur trim. Designed by **Chi Ling Moy** with a central slit to draw one end through for a snug fit around the neck.

KNITTED MEASUREMENTS

■ Approx 10½" x 35"/26.5cm x 89cm.

MATERIALS

■ 2 1¾oz/50g balls (each approx 280yd/255m) of Anny Blatt *Fine Kid* (wool/mohair ②) in #182 ecru (A)
■ 2yd/1m of Skacel Collection, Inc. Pelligo rabbit hair in tan (B)
■ One pair size 5 (3.5mm) needles *or size to obtain gauge*
■ One each sizes E/4 (3.5mm) and G/6 (4.5mm) crochet hooks

GAUGE

19 sts and 35 rows to 4"/10cm over seed st using 2 strands of yarn held tog and size 5 (3.5mm) needles.
Take time to check gauge.

Note Work with 2 strands of yarn held tog throughout.

SEED STITCH PATTERN

Over an odd number of sts.
Row 1 (RS) K1, *p1, k1; rep from * to end.
Rep row 1 for seed st pat. This stitch is reversible.

SCARF

With 2 strands of A and size 5 (3.5mm) needles, cast on 51 sts. Work in seed st pat for 8"/20.5cm.

Slit opening
Next row (RS) Work 18 sts in seed st, bind off center 15 sts for slit, work 18 sts in seed st.

Next row (WS) Work seed st to center bind off sts, with 2 strands of A, cast on 16 sts over these sts, then pass next st on LH needle over the last cast-on st (for a neat edge of opening), work seed st to end. Cont in seed st on all 51 sts until scarf measures 35"/89cm from beg. Bind off.

FINISHING

Block very lightly to measurements.
Fur trim edge
Row 1 (RS) With 1 strand A, and size E/4 (3.5mm) hook, work 1 sc in each st along one short end of scarf. Fasten off A.
Row 2 (RS) Join B to work row from RS, and with size G (4.5mm) hook, work 1 sc in each sc across. Fasten off B tightly. Cut end to approx 1"/2.5cm long to blend in with the fur edge (it is easier to cut the end instead of weaving it in which will cause extra bulk).

RIB AND STRIPE SCARF

It takes two

All of the colors in this easy striped scarf are present in one skein of yarn. The striping navigations are formed by alternating two separate balls at different color intervals. Designed by Kristin Spurkland.

KNITTED MEASUREMENTS

- Approx 7½" x 40"/19cm x 102cm

MATERIALS

- 3 1¾oz skeins (each approx 108yd/100m) of Noro/KFI *Kureyon* (wool③) in #95 green/peach multi
- One pair size 7 (4.5mm) needles *or size to obtain gauge*

GAUGE

23 sts and 27 rows to 4"/10cm over k3, p1 rib using size 7 (4.5mm) needles.
Take time to check gauge.

Note Stripe pattern is formed by alternating 2 separate balls of yarn every 2 rows, beg at different points of the color rep to give the multi stripe effect. Wind 2 skeins into 2 separate balls (balls A and B) and wind the 3rd skein into 2 more balls (balls A and B).

SCARF

Cast on 43 sts with ball A.

Row 1 (WS) With ball A, p3, *k1, p3; rep from * to end.

Row 2 (RS) With ball B, k3, *p1, k3; rep from * to end.

Row 3 With ball B, p3, *k1, p3; rep from * to end.

Row 4 With ball A, k3, *p1, k3; rep from * to end.

Rep these 4 rows for stripe pat until scarf measures approx 40"/102cm, ending with row 4 of color rib pat. Bind off in rib with A.

FINISHING

Block scarf lightly to measurements, being careful not to flatten rib.

An easy openwork stitch is worked using a featherweight hand dyed yarn combined with a larger needle to create this light and airy semi-transparent scarf. Designed by Karen Connor.

KNITTED MEASUREMENTS
- Approx 11½" x 60"/29cm x 152cm

MATERIALS
- 1 4oz/200g hank (each approx 1250yd/ 1153m) of Lorna's Laces *Helen's Lace* (silk/wool①) in #6NS Douglas fir
- One pair size 6 (4mm) needles *or size to obtain gauge*
- Size D/3 (3mm) crochet hook

GAUGE
24 sts and 32 rows to 4"/10cm over pat st using size 6 (4mm)needles.
Take time to check gauge.

PATTERN STITCH
(even number of sts)
Row 1 (RS) K1, *yo, k2tog; rep from *, end k1. Rep this row for pat st.

Note Due to the ability of this pattern stitch to stretch and lightweight yarn, the finished measurements should be determined by laying piece flat and pulling scarf in shape both widthwise and lengthwise.

SCARF
Cast on 68 sts loosely. Work in pat st until piece measures 60"/152cm from beg. Bind off loosely.

FINISHING
Block scarf to finished measurements.
Fringe
Cut a piece of cardboard to 9"/23cm on one side. Using this piece of cardboard, wind yarn 8-10 times around for each individual fringe. Cut one end of strands to form fringe. Slide crochet hook into space (from WS) at end of scarf and pull through looped end of fringe. Tighten to form a knot. Place 17 fringe at each end of scarf. Trim ends of fringe neatly.

Double knit rib squares in two colors are alternated with garter stitch squares in a separate color for a scarf style with double weight and dimension. Designed by Gayle Bunn.

KNITTED MEASUREMENTS

■ Approx 8" x 66"/20.5cm x 168cm

MATERIALS

■ 1 3½oz/100g ball (each approx 215yd/198m) each of Patons® *Classic Wool* (wool①) each in # 215 blue (A), #218 peacock (B) and #241 forest green (C)

■ One pair size 8 (5mm) needles *or size to obtain gauge*

GAUGE

18 sts and 32 rows to 4"/10cm over garter st using size 8 (5mm) needles.
Take time to check gauge.

STITCH GLOSSARY

K1 below K 1 st in row below st on needle at same time as slipping off the st from needle.

Notes

1 For easier working, wind small balls of yarn for each block of color for completing a row of blocks. Twist yarns tog when changing colors.

2 Foll diagram as a guide for the color placement of entire scarf.

SCARF

With A, cast on 13 sts; then cont with B, cast on 13 sts; then cont with C, cast on 13 sts—39 sts total.

Beg Patchwork Pat

Row 1 (RS) With C, k13; with B, k13; with A, k13.

Row 2 With A, [p1, k1 below] 6 times, p1; with B, [p1, k1 below] 6 times, p1; with C, k13.

Rows 3-24 Rep rows 1 and 2 11 times more.

Row 25 (RS) With A, k13; with C, k13; with B, k13.

Row 26 With B, [p1, k1 below] 6 times, p1; with C, k13; with A, [p1, k1 below] 6 times, p1.

Rows 27-48 Rep rows 25 and 26 11 times more.

Row 49 (RS) With B, k13; with A, k13; with C, k13.

Row 50 With C, k13; with A, [p1, k1 below] 6 times, p1; with B, [p1, k1 below] 6 times, p1.

Rows 51-72 Rep rows 49 and 50 11 times more.

Rep these 72 rows a total of 7 times (see

chart). Then, work rows 1-24 once more.
Bind off all sts.

FINISHING

Block very lightly (although blocking may
be unnecessary due to the nature of the st
patterns).

Fringe

Cut A, B and C into 12"/30.5cm lengths.
Taking 4 strands tog for each fringe and
folding in half, work 6 fringe in each
square matching colors of scarf squares.

COLOR PLACEMENT DIAGRAM

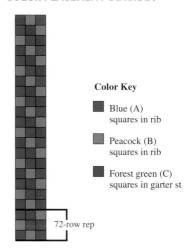

Color Key

■ Blue (A)
squares in rib

■ Peacock (B)
squares in rib

■ Forest green (C)
squares in garter st

72-row rep

A base knit triangle is worked in garter stitch using a variety of color combinations to create this angled-ended scarf. The triangles are then joined together in this design by Jacqueline Jewett.

KNITTED MEASUREMENTS

■ Approx 6"/15cm wide and 52"/132cm long at longest point and 39"/99cm long at shortest point

MATERIALS

■ 1 3½oz/100g ball (each approx 254yd/229m) of Brown Sheep Yarn Company *Nature Spun Worsted Weight* (wool④) each in #601 black (A), #101 rust (B), #308 gold (C), # 730 white (D), #N85 dk pink (E), N98 pink (F), and #N06 berry (G)

■ One pair size 7 (4.5mm) needles *or size to obtain gauge*

GAUGE

■ 20 sts and 40 rows to 4"/10cm over garter st using size 7 (4.5mm) needles.

■ One triangle measures 13"/33cm at widest point and 6"/15cm high at center. *Take time to check gauge.*

NOTE

Work colors as designated for each triangle or in a random striping pattern as desired.

BASE TRIANGLE

With designated color, cast on 89 sts.

Row 1 (RS) K43, k3tog, k43—87 sts.

Row 2 Knit.

Row 3 K2tog, k40, k3tog, k40, k2tog—83 sts.

Row 4 Knit.

Row 5 K2tog, k38, k3tog, k38, k2tog—79 sts.

Row 6 Knit.

Row 7 K2tog, k36, k3tog, k36, k2tog—75 sts.

Row 8 Knit. Cont to dec in this way working a k2tog at beg and end of every other row and a k3tog at center of this row until 7 sts rem and 42 rows have been worked.

Row 43 K2tog, k3tog, k2tog—3 sts.

Row 44 Knit.

Row 45 K3tog and fasten off.

SCARF

Work 7 triangles foll pattern of base triangle and layout foll diagram.

Triangle 1

Work 2 rows black (A), 6 rows rust (B), 4 rows gold (C), 2 rows black (A), 2 rows white (D), 4 rows dk pink (E), 6 rows pink (F), 2 rows black (A), 4 rows berry (G), 2 rows white (D), 2 rows dk pink (E), 6 rows gold (C), 3 rows black (A).

Triangle 2

Work 2 rows berry (G), 2 rows white (D), 6 rows gold (C), 2 rows black (A), 4 rows dk pink (E), 2 rows white (D), 6 rows rust

(B), 4 rows pink (F), 2 rows black (A), 2 rows dk pink (E), 6 rows berry (G), 4 rows gold (C), 3 rows black (A).

Triangle 3

Work 2 rows white (D), 2 rows black (A), 6 rows pink (F), 4 rows dk pink (E), 2 rows berry (G), 2 rows white (D), 6 rows rust (B), 2 rows gold (C), 2 rows black (A), 4 rows gold (C), 2 rows white (D), 4 rows dk pink (E), 4 rows berry (G), 3 rows black (A).

Triangle 4

Work 2 rows black (A), 6 rows pink (F), 4 rows dk pink (E), 2 rows white (D), 2 rows black (A), 2 rows gold (C), 2 rows black (A), 6 rows berry (G), 2 rows white (D), 2 rows black (A), 4 rows gold (C), 4 rows rust (B), 2 rows white (D), 2 rows dk pink (E), 3 rows black (A).

Triangle 5

Work 2 rows gold (C), 6 rows berry (G), 2 rows white (D), 2 rows black (A), 6 rows dk pink (E), 2 rows pink (F), 2 rows berry (G), 4 rows pink (F), 2 rows black (A), 2 rows white (D), 4 rows rust (B), 2 rows gold (C), 2 rows berry (G), 4 rows pink (F), 3 rows black (A).

Triangle 6

Work 2 rows black (A), 4 rows dk pink (E), 2 rows white (D), 6 rows berry (G), 4 rows gold (C), 2 rows black (A), 2 rows pink (F), 4 rows dk pink (E), 2 rows white (D), 6 rows rust (B), 2 rows black (A), 2 rows white (D), 4 rows gold (C), 3 rows black (A).

Triangle 7

Work 2 rows dk pink (E), 2 rows black (A), 6 rows pink (F), 2 rows berry (G), 2 rows white (D), 2 rows dk pink (E), 4 rows gold (C), 2 rows black (A), 2 rows white (D), 6 rows rust (B), 2 rows white (D), 4 rows dk pink (E), 2 rows black (A), 2 rows gold (C), 2 rows berry (G), 3 rows black (A).

FINISHING

Block pieces lightly to measurements. Layout foll diagram. Sew each triangle tog forming scarf by using overcast st and matching colors.

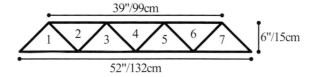

WOVEN PATTERN SCARF

Autumn sonata

One hank of bulky weight yarn knits up into a simple flat fabric design for this ombre hued scarf. Designed by Irina Poludnenko.

KNITTED MEASUREMENTS
- Approx 7½" x 60"/19cm x 152cm

MATERIALS
- 1 8oz/250g hank (approx 244yd/225m) of Cherry Tree Hill Yarn *14 Ply* (wool⑤) in Indian summer
- One pair size 11 (8mm) needles or size to obtain gauge

GAUGE
12 sts and 24 rows to 4"/10cm over woven pat st using size 11 (8mm) needles.
Take time to check gauge.

WOVEN PATTERN STITCH

(Multiple of 4 sts plus 2)
Row 1 (RS) Sl 1 st, *k2, sl 2 sts wyif; rep from * to last st, p1.
Row 2 Sl 1 st, *sl 2 sts wyib, p2; rep from *, end p1.
Row 3 Sl 1 st, *sl 2 sts wyif, k2; rep from *, end p1.
Row 4 Sl 1 st, *p2, sl 2 sts wyib; rep from *, end p1.
Rep rows 1-4 for woven pat st.

SCARF

Cast on 26 sts. Work in pat st until scarf measures approx 60"/152cm. Fasten off.

FINISHING

Block lightly to measurements (do not press).

Fringe
For each fringe, cut 3 strands each 9"/23cm long. Pull 7 fringe through each lower edge of scarf.

Very Easy Very Vogue

The changing of colors down the center and a switch over from right side to wrong side make this scarf style truly reversible. Designed by Julie Mach.

KNITTED MEASUREMENTS

- Approx 8½" x 72"/21.5cm x 183cm

MATERIALS

- 2 3½oz/100g balls (each approx 183yd/167m) of Tahki Yarns/Tahki•Stacy Charles, Inc. *Donegal Tweed* (wool④) each in #815 navy tweed (A) and #803 green tweed (B)
- One pair size 10 (6mm) needles *or size to obtain gauge*

GAUGE

15 sts and 28 rows to 4"/10cm over garter st stripe pat using size 10 (6mm) needles. *Take time to check gauge.*

Note All color changes are made at the center of the scarf to make scarf reversible.

Be sure to twist yarns every row on the side that is not facing (or the back side of the work).

SCARF

With A, cast on 16 sts, then cont with B, cast on 16 sts—32 sts total.

Row 1 (RS) Knit across all 32 sts with B, twisting yarns tog at center of scarf.

Row 2 K16 sts with B, drop B and K16 with A.

Row 3 Knit across all 32 sts with A, twisting yarns tog at center of scarf.

Row 4 K16 sts with A, drop A and k16 with B.

Rep rows 1-4 for garter st stripe pat until piece measures 72"/183cm from beg. Bind off.

FINISHING

Block lightly to measurements.

Fringe

Cut 3 strands of one color for each fringe, each 10¼"/26cm long. Alternating colors A and B, pull through 31 fringe on each end of scarf.

For Intermediate Knitters

This lightweight neck warmer is ideally suited for both men and women. An easy two-row pattern forms the base of the chevron pattern with maximum visual appeal. Designed by Betty Monroe.

KNITTED MEASUREMENTS
- Approx 7¼" x 45¼"/18.5cm x 115cm

MATERIALS
- 2 1¾oz/50g balls (each approx 227yd/210m) of Schoeller Esslinger/Skacel *Fortissima* (wool/polyamide②) in #184 dk grey (MC)
- 1 ball each in #60 grey tweed (A), #1011 wine (B), #123 lt grey (C), #9480 hot pink (D) and #9418 med blue (E)
- One pair size 3 (3.25mm) needles *or size to obtain gauge*
- Size 3 (3.25mm) circular needle, 29"/74cm long

GAUGE
30 sts and 40 rows to 4"/10cm over St st using size 3 (3.25mm) needles.
Take time to check gauge.

Note Take gauge over St st instead of the chevron pat st to properly determine gauge suitable for the pattern st.

CHEVRON PATTERN STITCH
Row 1 (RS) K2, k2tog, *k6, yo, k1, yo, k6, SK2P; rep from * once, end k6, yo, k1, yo, k6, ssk, k2.
Row 2 Purl.
Rep these 2 rows for chevron pat st.

SCARF
With straight needles and MC, cast on 53 sts.
Preparation rows
Rows 1 and 2 Knit.
Then, cont in chevron pat st, work stripes as foll: 4 rows MC, * 2 rows A, 2 rows B, 2 rows A, 2 rows C, 2 rows A, 2 rows D, 2 rows A, 6 rows MC, 2 rows E *, 6 rows MC. Rep between *'s once. Then cont as foll: ** 28 rows MC, 2 rows E **; rep between **'s 7 times more. Then work *6 rows MC, 2 rows A, 2 rows D, 2 rows A, 2 rows C, 2 rows A, 2 rows B, 2 rows A *, 6 rows MC, 2 rows E. Rep between *'s once. Work 4 rows MC. K2 rows with MC. Bind off knitwise.

FINISHING
Block scarf to measurements.
Side edging
Working into the space between the first and 2nd sts along one edge (that is, covering the first or end st), with RS facing, circular needle and MC, pick up and k sts as foll: * pick up and k3 sts, skip 1 st, pick up and k2 sts, skip 1 st; rep from * to other end. Knit 2 rows. Bind off knitwise. Rep edging on other long edge.

NOTES

NOTES

RESOURCES

Write to the yarn companies listed below for purchasing and mail-order information.

ADRIAFIL
distributed by
Plymouth Yarn

ARTFUL YARNS
distributed by
JCA

ANNY BLATT/BOUTON D'OR
7796 Boardwalk
Brighton, MI 48116

BERROCO, INC.
PO Box 367
Uxbridge, MA 01569

BLUE SKY ALPACA
PO Box 387
St. Francis, MN 55070

BROWN SHEEP CO.
100662 County Road 16
Mitchell, NE 69357

CHERRY TREE HILL, INC.
PO Box 659
Barton, VT 05822

CLASSIC ELITE YARNS
300A Jackson Street
Lowell, MA 01852

COLINETTE YARNS
distributed by
Unique Kolours

CRYSTAL PALACE
2320 Bissell Avenue
Richmond, CA 94804

FILATURA DI CROSA
distributed by
Tahki•Stacy Charles, Inc.

GGH
distributed by
Muench Yarns

JCA
35 Scales Lane
Townsend, MA 01469

KNIT ONE CROCHET TOO
7 Commons Ave., Suite 2
Windham, ME 04062

KNITTING FEVER, INC.
PO Box 502
Roosevelt, NY 11575

LANE BORGOSESIA
distributed by
Trendsetter Yarns

LORNA'S LACES YARNS
4229 N. Honore St.
Chicago, IL 60613

MUENCH YARNS
285 Bel Marin Keys Blvd.
Unit J
Novato, CA 94949-5724

NATURALLY
distributed
S. R. Kertzer, Ltd.

NORO
distributed by
KFI

PATONS®
PO Box 40
Listowel, ON
N4W 3H3
Canada

PLYMOUTH YARN
PO Box 28
Bristol, PA 19007

ROWAN YARNS
4 Townsend West, Suite 8
Nashua, NH 03063

S. R. KERTZER, LTD.
105A Winges Road
Woodbridge, ON L4L 6C2
Canada

SCHOELLER ESSLINGER
distirbuted by
Skacel Collection

SKACEL COLLECTION
PO Box 88110
Seattle, WA 98138-2110

TAHKI YARNS
distributed by
Tahki•Stacy Charles, Inc.

TAHKI•STACY CHARLES, INC.
8000 Cooper Ave.
Glendale, NY 11385

TRENDSETTER YARNS
16745 Saticoy St. #101
Van Nuys, CA 91406

UNIQUE KOLOURS
1428 Oak Lane
Downingtown, PA 19335

*Write to US resources for
mail-order availability
of yarns not listed.*

BERROCO, INC.
distributed by
S. R. Kertzer, Ltd.

CLASSIC ELITE YARNS
distributed by
S. R. Kertzer, Ltd.

DIAMOND YARN
9697 St. Laurent
Montreal, PQ H3L 2N1
and
155 Martin Ross, Unit #3
Toronto, ON M3J 2L9

LES FILS MUENCH
5640 Rue Valcourt
Brossard, Quebec J4W1C5

NATURALLY
distributed by
S. R. Kertzer, Ltd.

PATONS®
PO Box 40
Listowel, ON N4W 3H3

ROWAN
distributed by
Diamond Yarn

S. R. KERTZER, LTD.
105A Winges Rd.
Woodbridge, ON L4L 6C2

SCHOELLER ESSLINGER
distributed by
Diamond Yarn

---

*Not all yarns used in this
book are available in
the UK. For yarns not
available, make a
comparable substitute or
contact the US manufacturer
for purchasing and
mail-order information.*

COLINETTE YARNS
Units 2-5
Banwy Workshops
Llanfair Caereinion
Powys SY21 0SG
Tel: 01938-810128

ROWAN YARNS
Green Lane Mill
Holmfirth
West Yorks HD7 1RW
Tel: 01484-681881

SILKSTONE
12 Market Place
Cockermouth
Cumbria, CA13 9NQ
Tel: 01900-821052

**THOMAS RAMSDEN
GROUP**
Netherfield Road
Guiseley
West Yorks LS20 9PD
Tel: 01943-872264

VOGUE KNITTING SCARVES TWO

Editorial Director
TRISHA MALCOLM

Yarn Editor
VERONICA MANNO

Art Director
CHI LING MOY

Editorial Coordinator
MICHELLE LO

Executive Editor
CARLA S. SCOTT

Photography
JACK DEUTSCH STUDIOS

Instructions Editor
MARI LYNN PATRICK

Book Publishing Coordinator
CARA BECKERICH

Patterns Editor
KAREN GREENWALD

Production Manager
DAVID JOINNIDES

Knitting Editor
JEAN GUIRGUIS

President, Sixth&Spring Books
ART JOINNIDES

LOOK FOR THESE OTHER TITLES IN THE *VOGUE KNITTING ON THE GO!* SERIES...

BABY BLANKETS

SCARVES

BABY GIFTS

SOCKS

BABY KNITS

SOCKS TWO

BAGS & BACKPACKS

TEEN KNITS

CAPS & HATS

TODDLER KNITS

CAPS & HATS TWO

VESTS

CHUNKY KNITS

VINTAGE KNITS

KIDS KNITS

WEEKEND KNITS

MITTENS & GLOVES

BEGINNER BASICS

PILLOWS